A Look
at three
pages
inside.

A Look at three pages inside.

A Look at three pages inside.

Get creative with these
vintage toy cars
that found their way
to me after being
stored in a box

in a shed
somewhere

just
outside
New Orleans!
I cleaned them

up the best I
could and then
photographed

them in different
positions.
I have quite a few more
to do....so watch for book two!

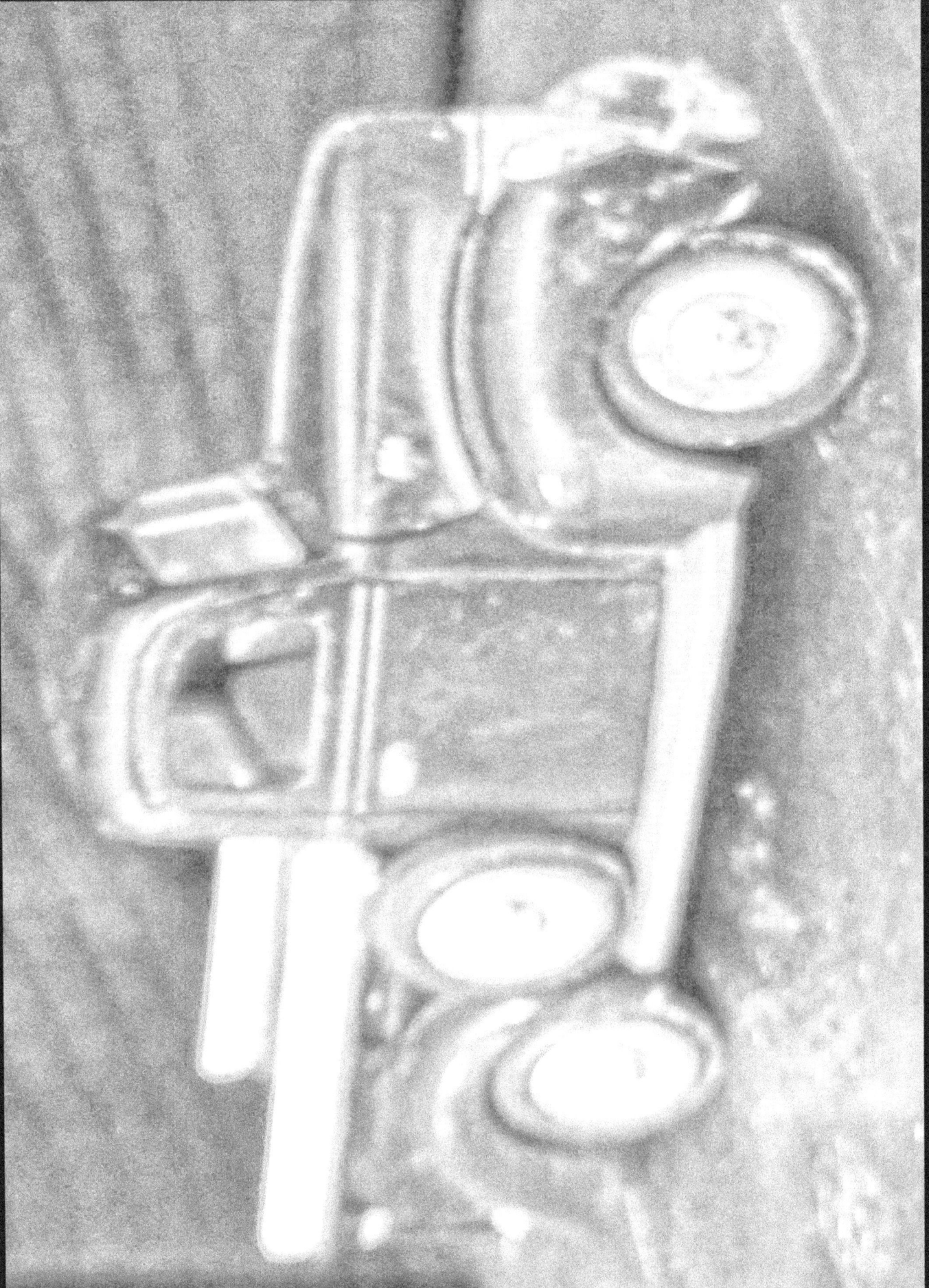

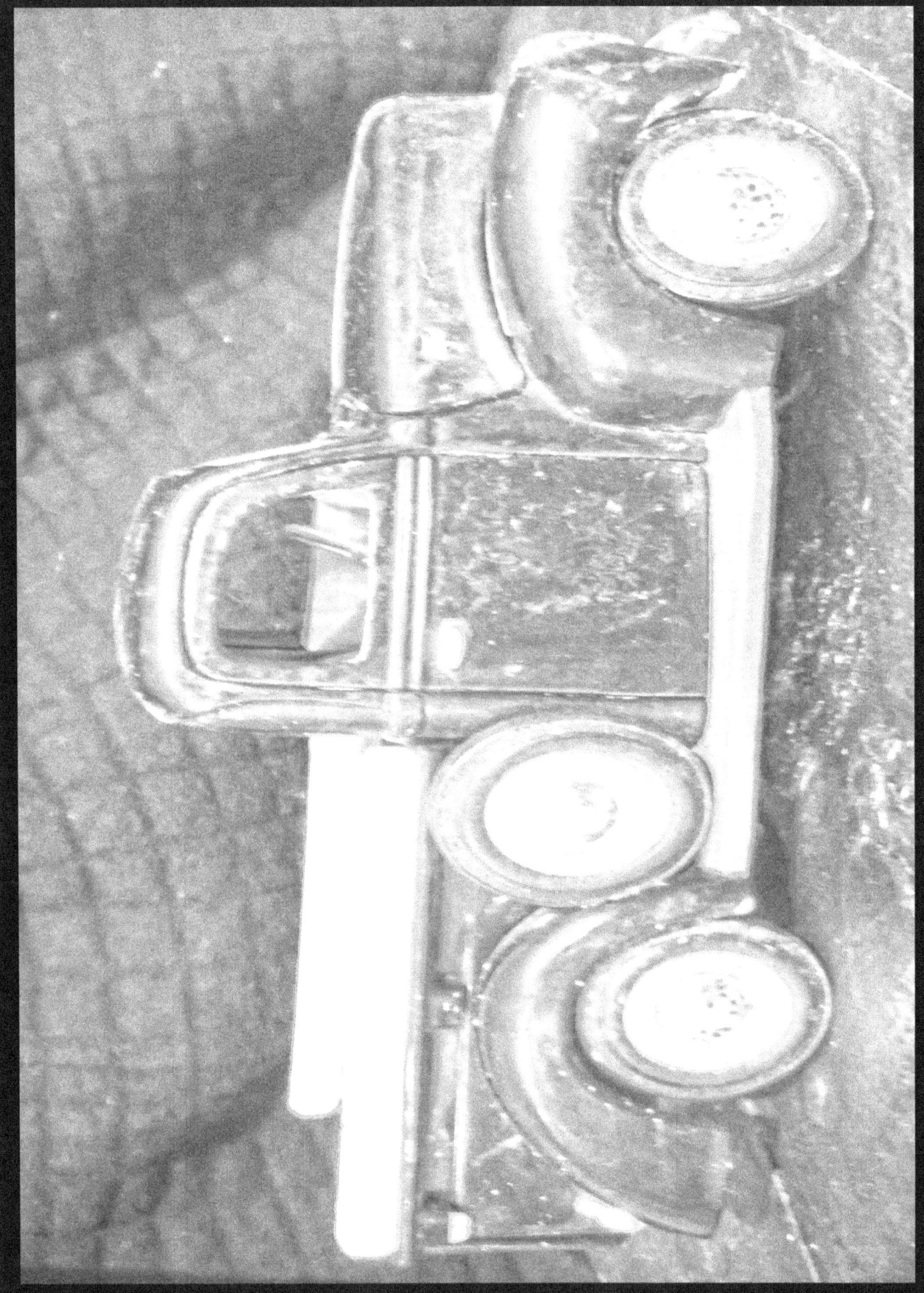

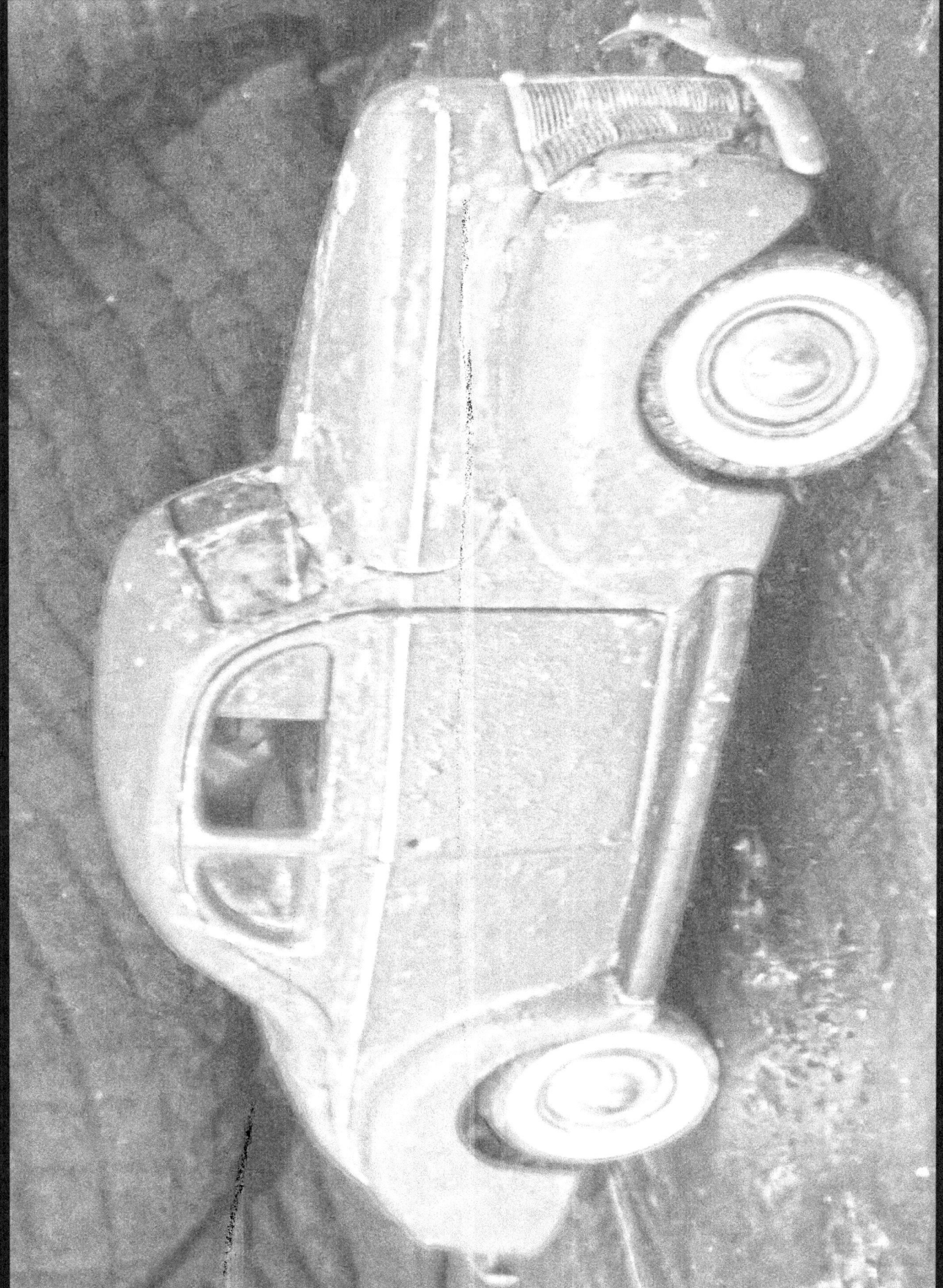

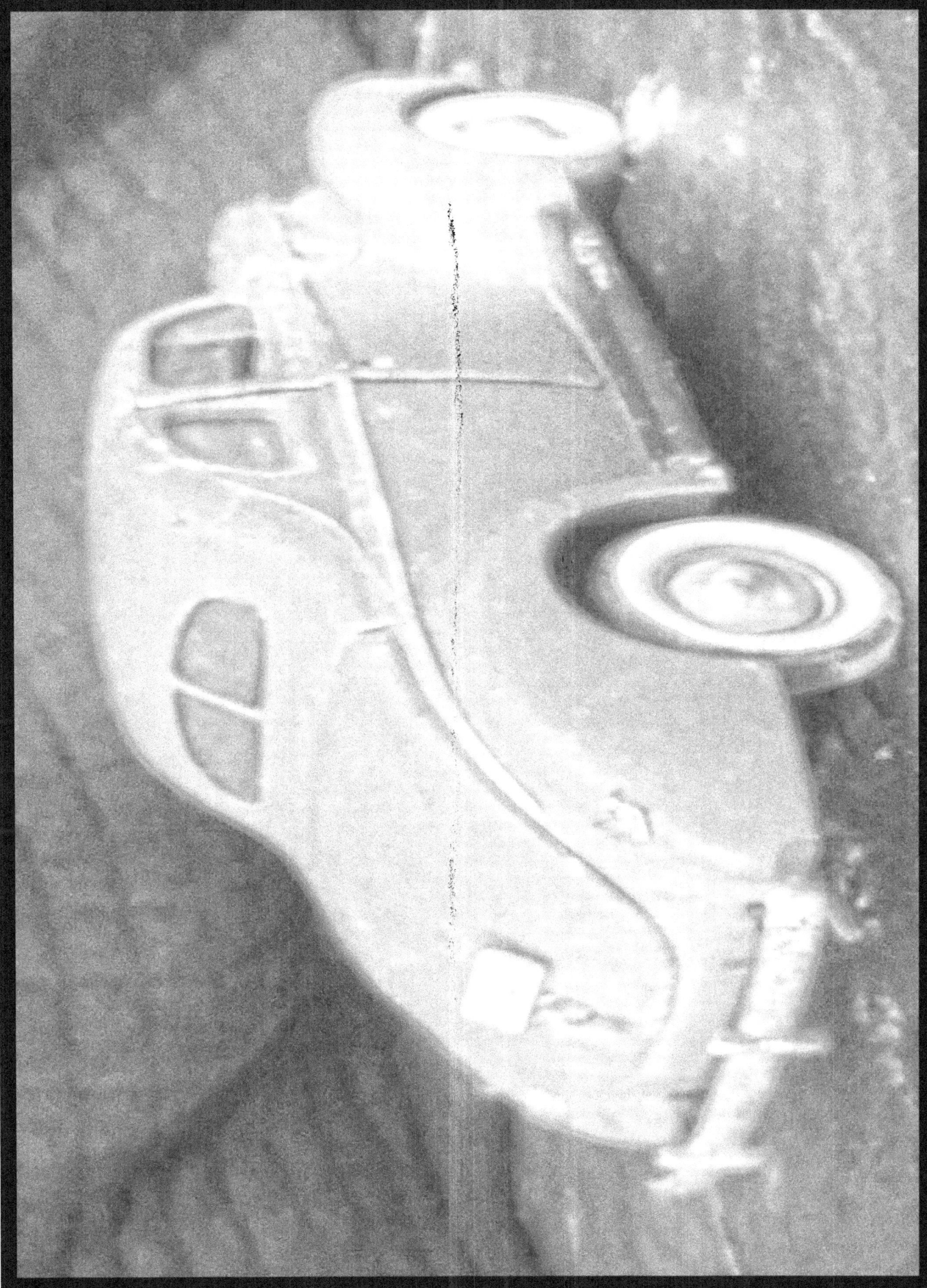

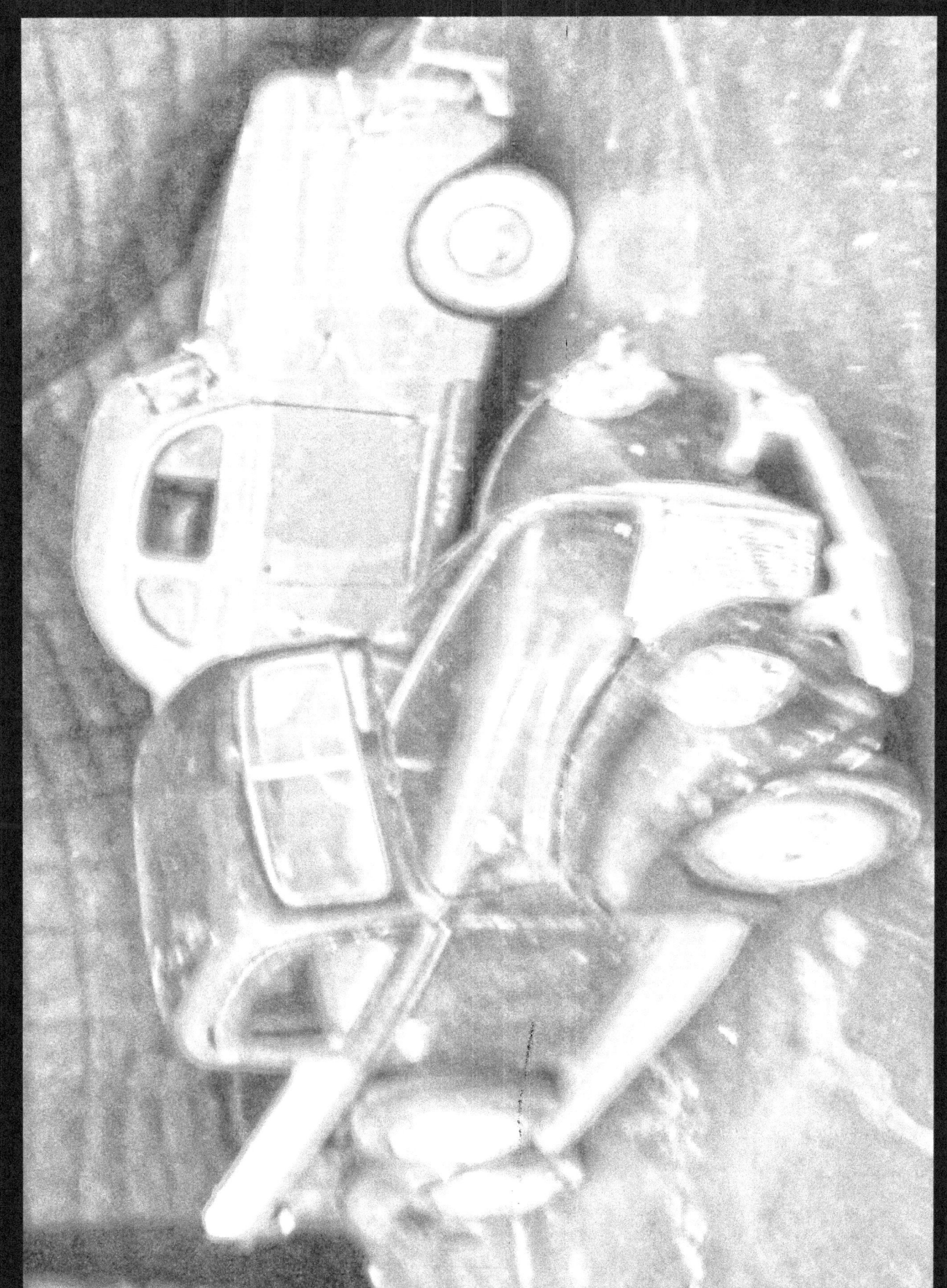

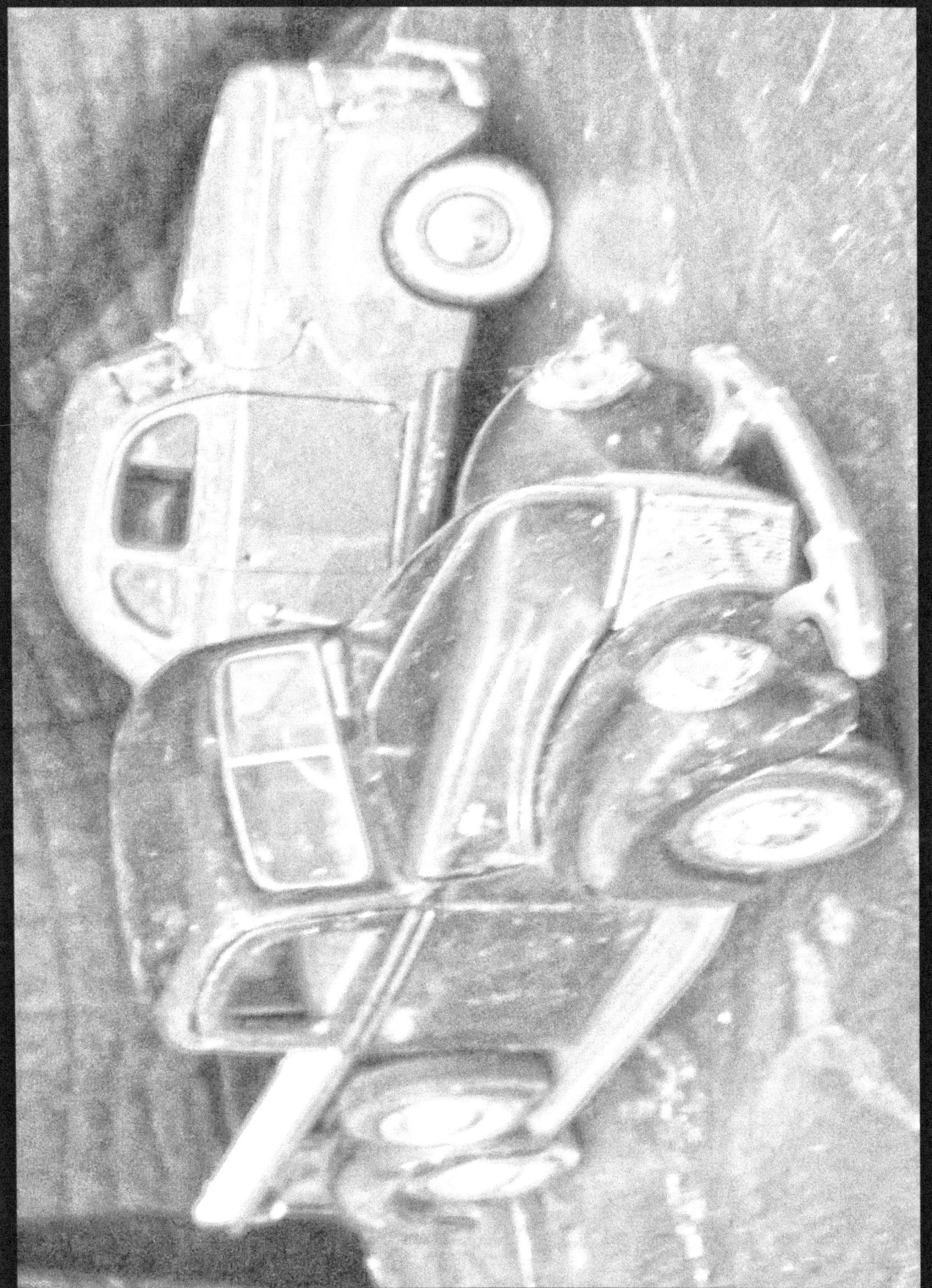

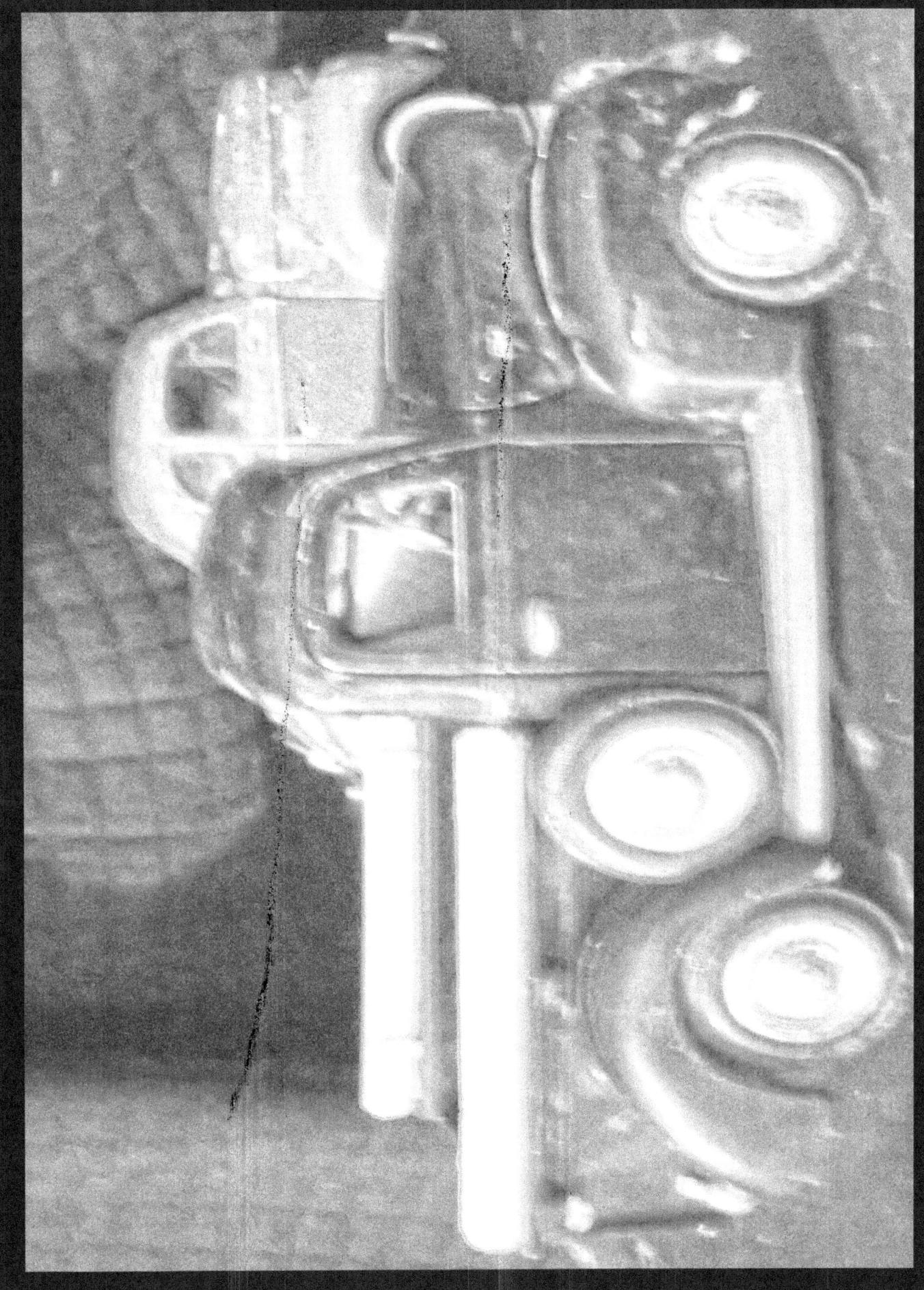

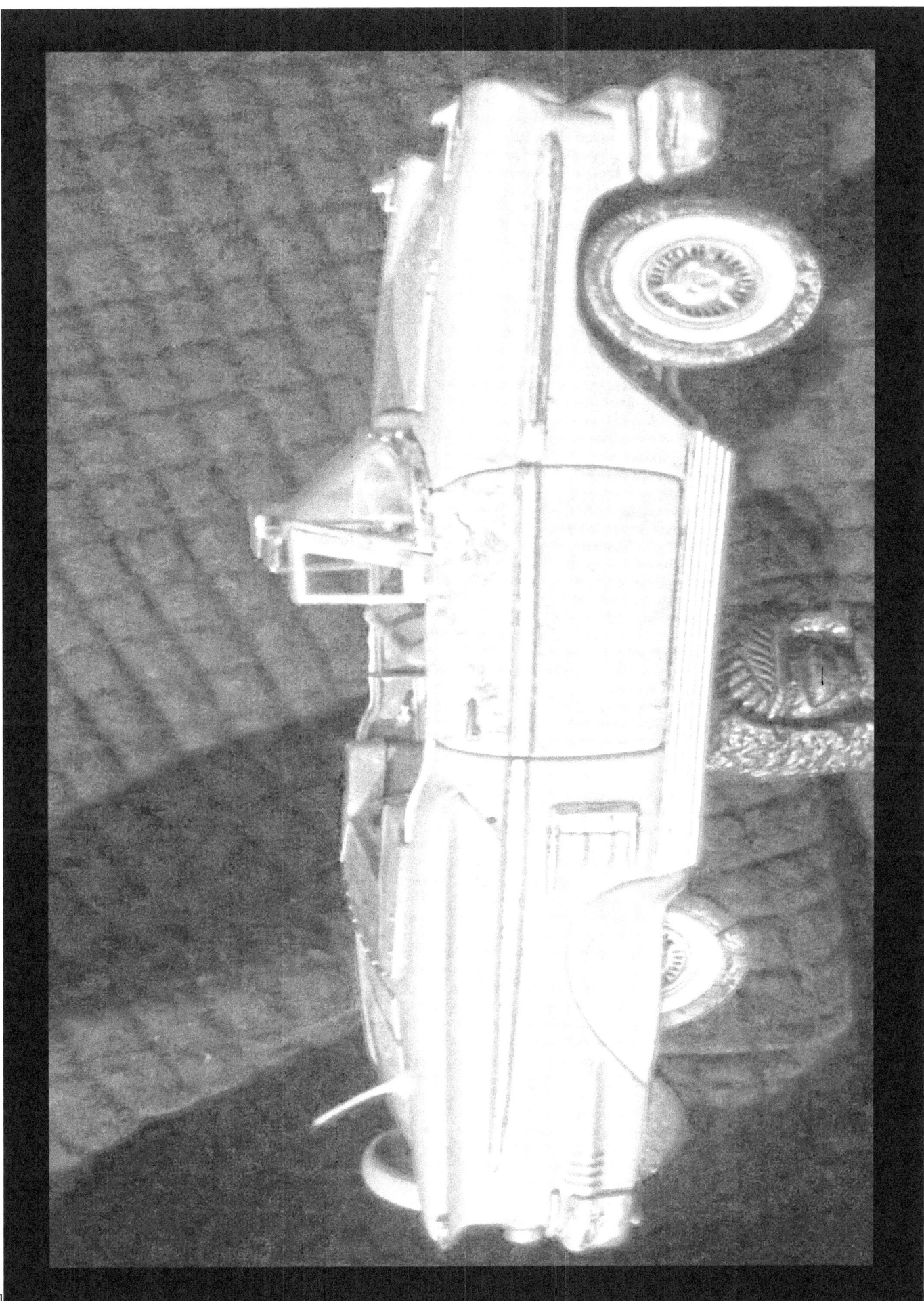

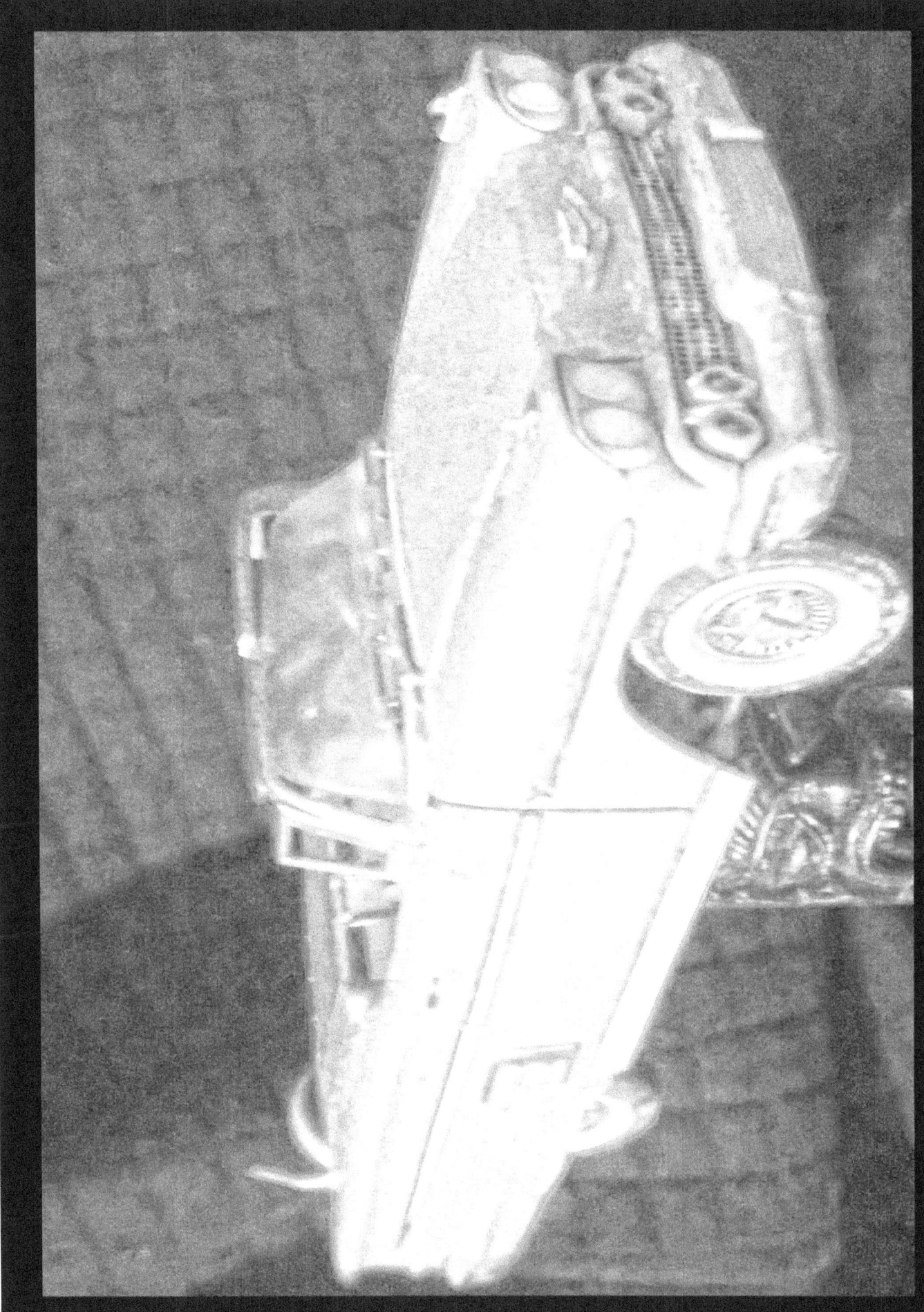

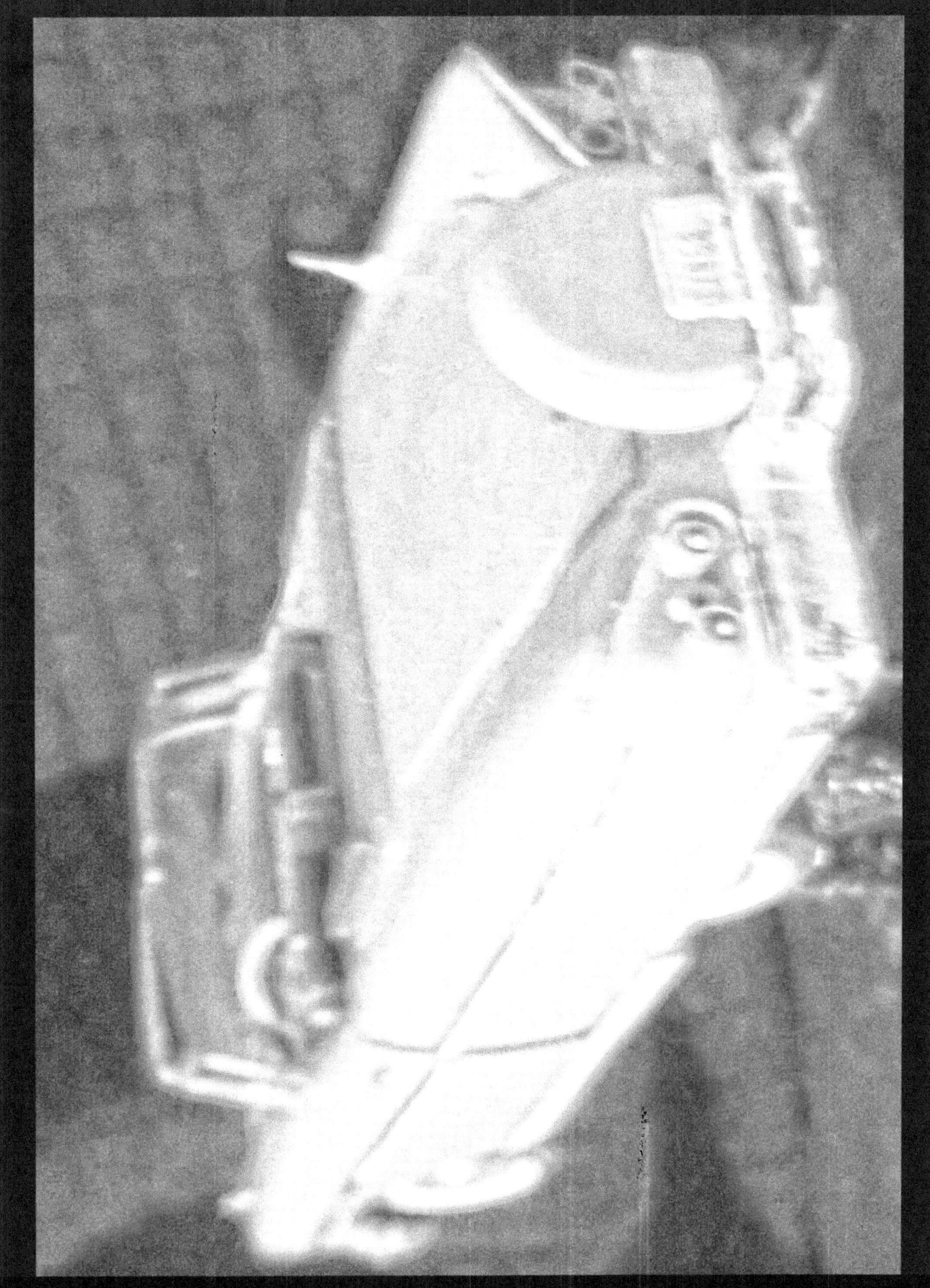

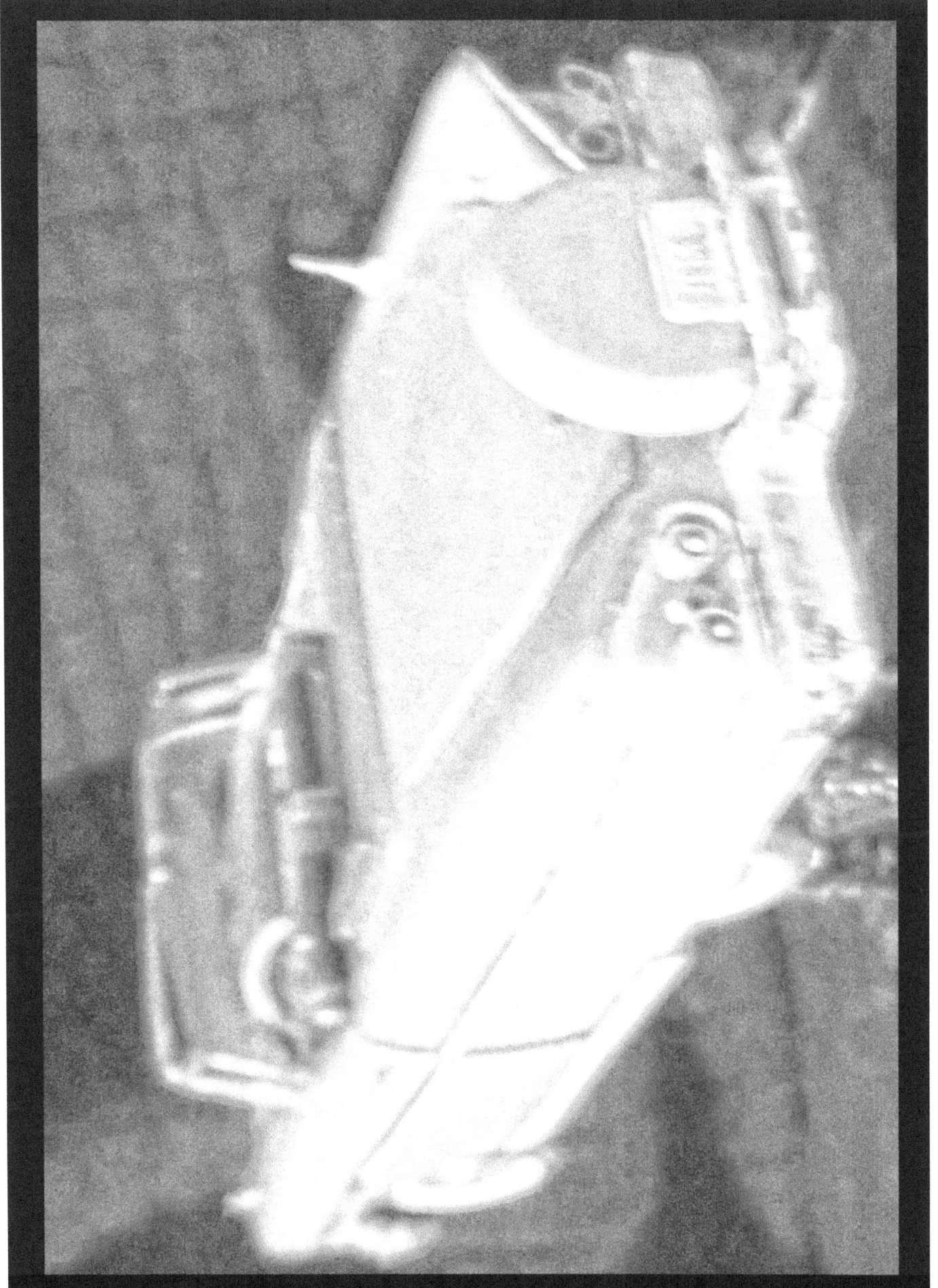

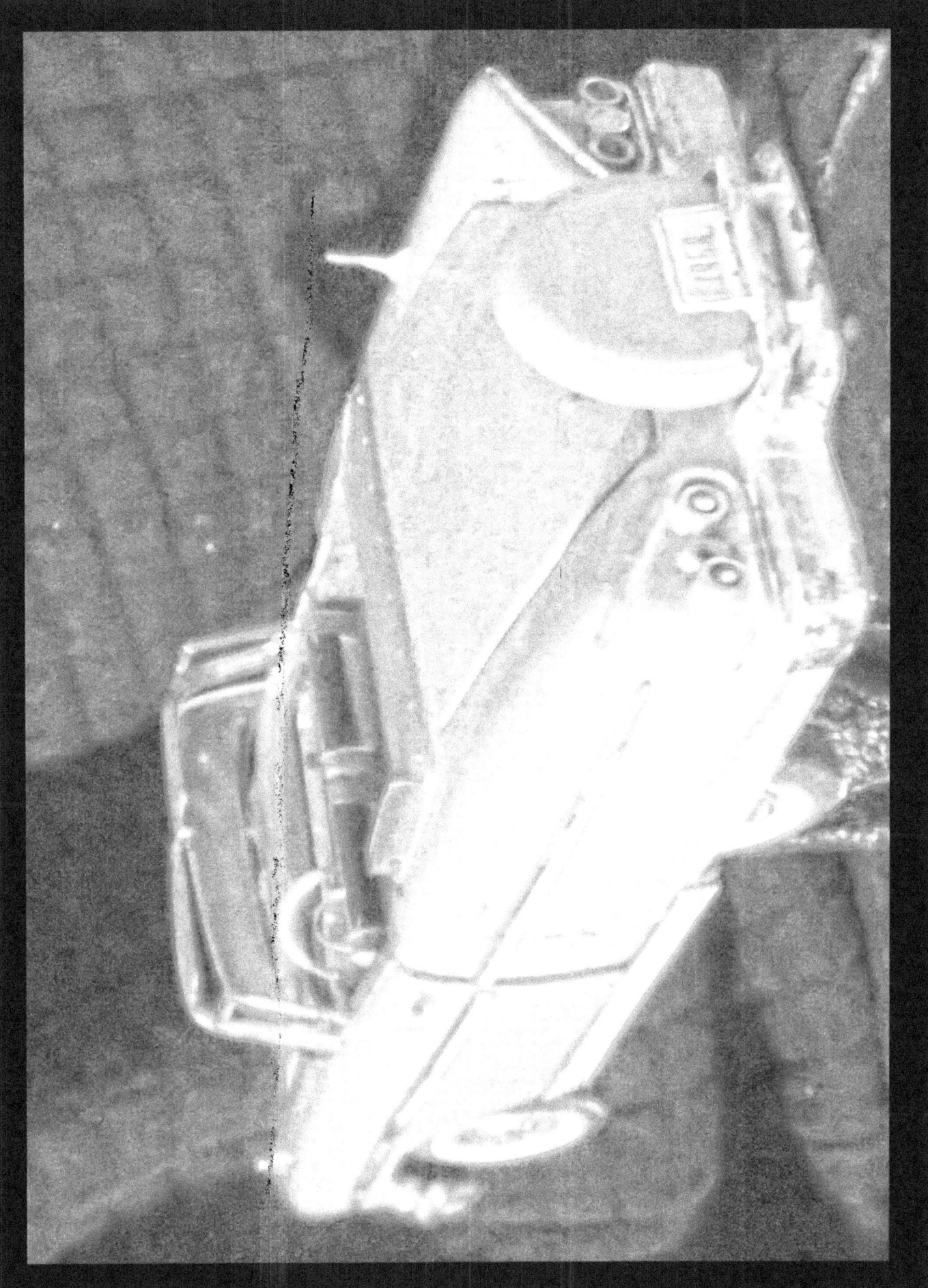

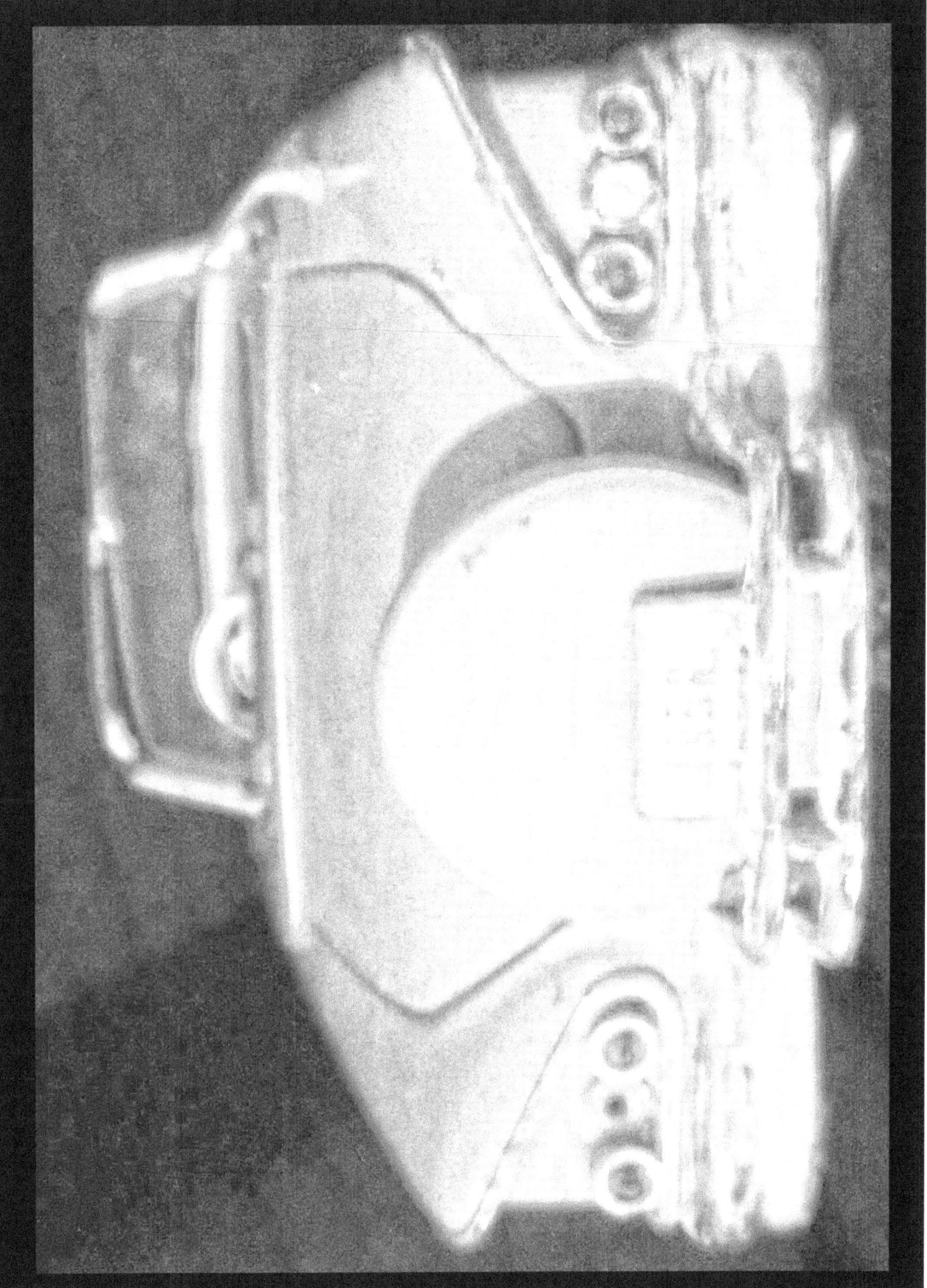

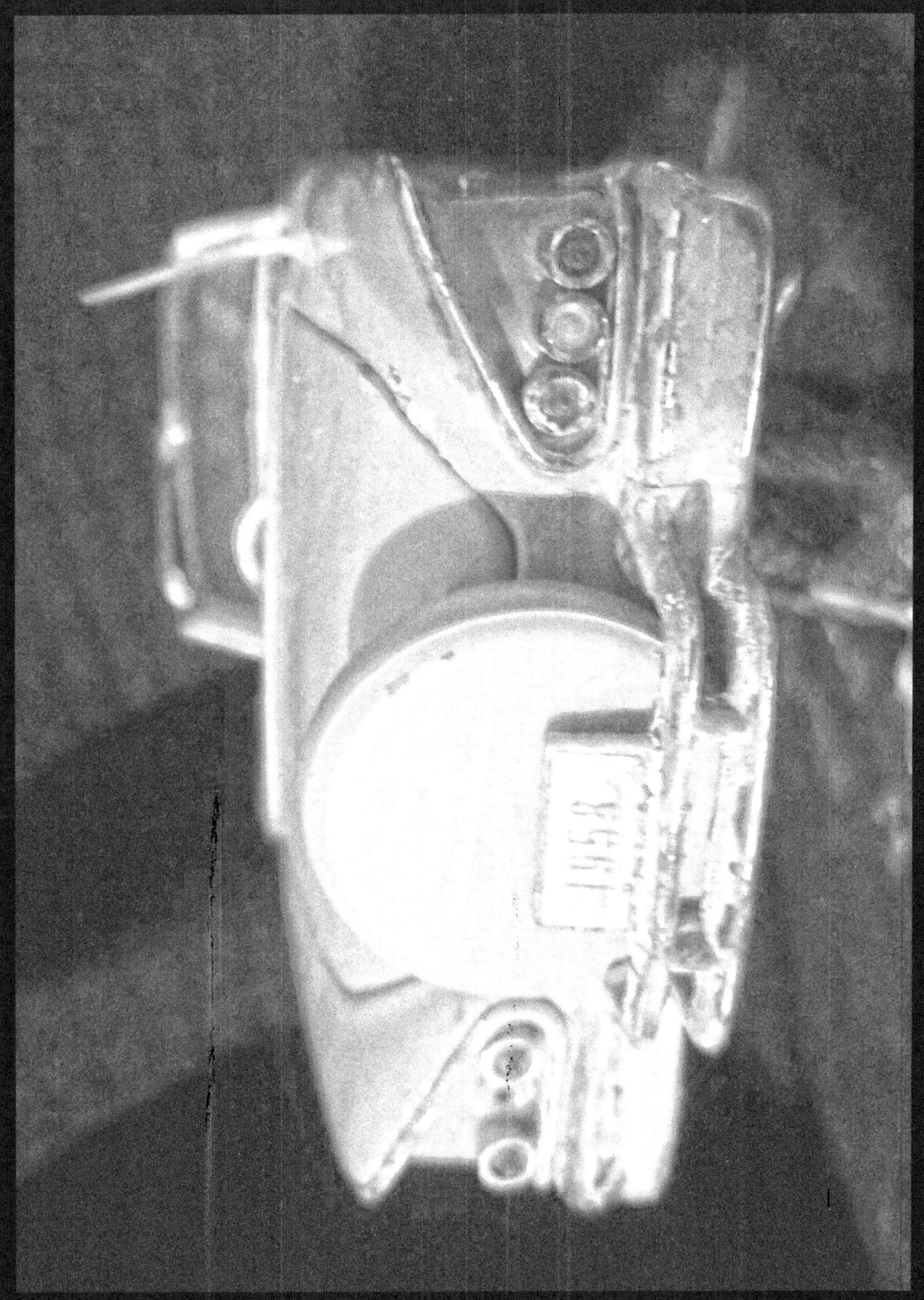

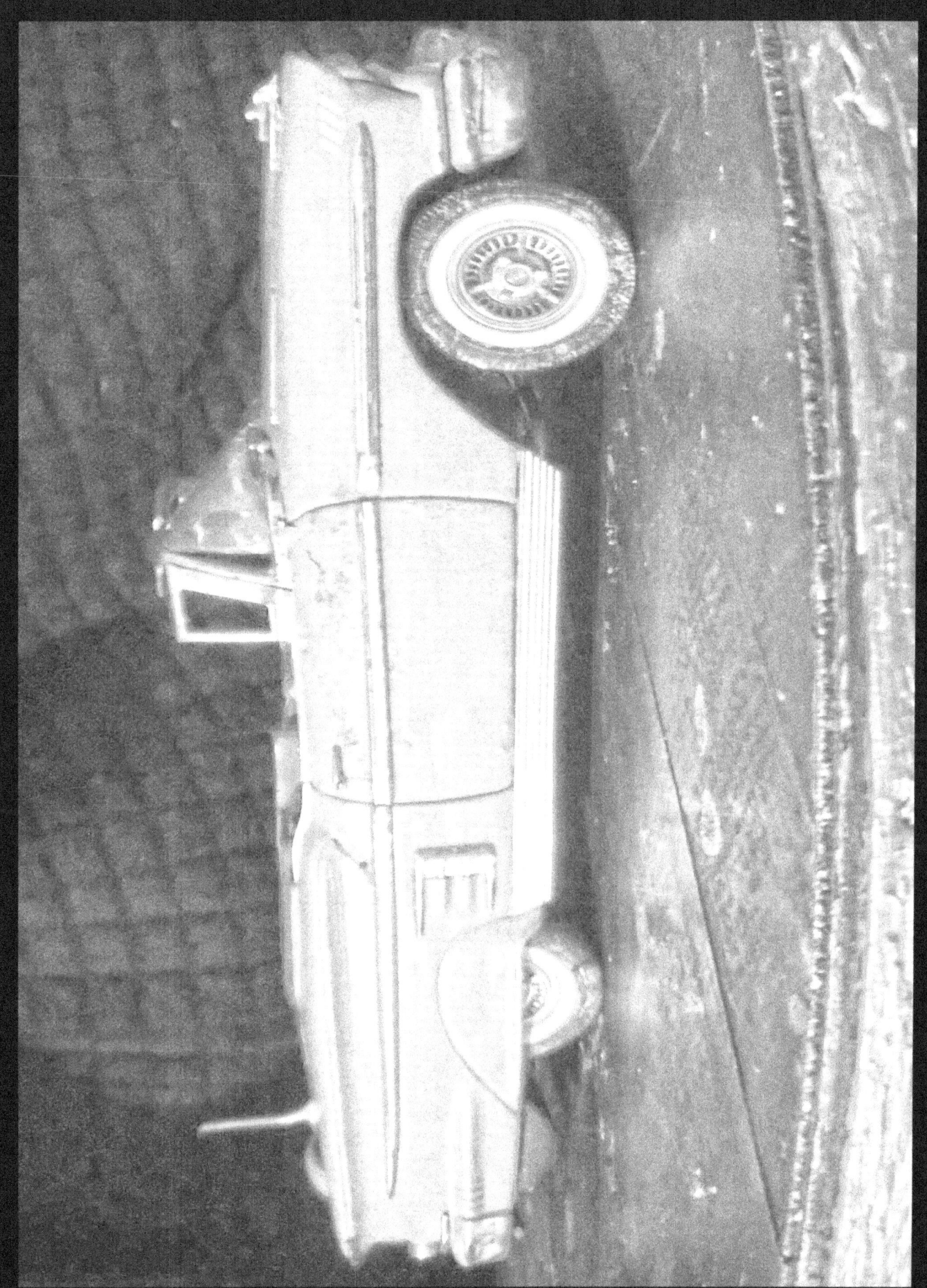

A Look
at three
pages
inside.

A Look at three pages inside.